Athletes Who Made a Difference

SIMONE BILES

Josh Anderson

illustrated by Casey Ella Fredrick

Graphic Universe™ • Minneapolis

Graphic Universe™
An imprint of Lerner Publishing Group, Inc.
241 First Avenue North
Minneapolis, MN 55401 USA

For reading levels and more information, look up this title at www.lernerbooks.com.

Main body text set in CCDaveGibbonsLower
Typeface provided by Comicraft

Photo Acknowledgments
The images in this book are used with the permission of: © Jamie Squire/Staff/Getty Images, p. 28 (left); © SAUL LOEB/Contributor/Getty Images, p. 28 (right).

Library of Congress Cataloging-in-Publication Data

Names: Anderson, Josh, author. | Fredrick, Casey Ella, illustrator.
Title: Simone Biles : athletes who made a difference / Josh Anderson ; [illustrated by Casey Ella Fredrick].
Description: Minneapolis, MN : Graphic Universe, [2024] | Series: Athletes who made a difference | Includes
    bibliographical references and index. | Audience: Ages 8–12 years | Audience: Grades 4–6 | Summary: "Despite
    only being 27 years old, Simone Biles has earned the Presidential Medal of Freedom and a world–record tying 32
    combined Olympic and World Championship medals. This is her story"—Provided by publisher.
Identifiers: LCCN 2023049774 (print) | LCCN 2023049775 (ebook) | ISBN 9781728492988 (library binding) |
    ISBN 9798765628027 (paperback) | ISBN 9798765631331 (epub)
Subjects: LCSH: Biles, Simone 1997-—Juvenile literature. | Women gymnasts—United States—Biography—Juvenile
    literature. | African American women athletes—United States—Biography—Juvenile literature. | African American
    women Olympic athletes—United States—Biography—Juvenile literature. | Olympic Games (31st : 2016 : Rio de
    Janeiro, Brazil)—Juvenile literature. | Presidential Medal of Freedom—Juvenile literature.
Classification: LCC GV460.2.B55 A53 2024 (print) | LCC GV460.2.B55 (ebook) | DDC 796.44092 [B]—dc23/
    eng/20231213

LC record available at https://lccn.loc.gov/2023049774
LC ebook record available at https://lccn.loc.gov/2023049775

Manufactured in the United States of America
1 – CG – 7/15/24

Table of Contents

CHAPTER 1

A STAR IS BORN

Simone Biles was born on March 14, 1997, in Columbus, Ohio. She had two older siblings, Tevi and Ashley.

Simone's mom struggled with addiction. Her dad was not around. Simone and her siblings spent a lot of their early lives in foster homes. In 1999, Simone's younger sister Adria was born.

When Simone was six and Adria was four, they were adopted by their grandparents. The sisters moved to the suburbs near Houston, Texas. Their grandparents provided a stable and loving home for the girls.

In 2003, six-year-old Simone's class took a field trip to a gymnastics center.

This is fun!

I think I can do that.

I can do it!

Simone fell in love with gymnastics. She began training regularly with coach Aimee Boorman. They worked hard at all four competitive women's events.

Boorman saw great potential in her student. Simone had great natural strength. But flexibility and finesse were necessary too. Boorman's coaching focused on preparing Simone to become a great all-around gymnast.

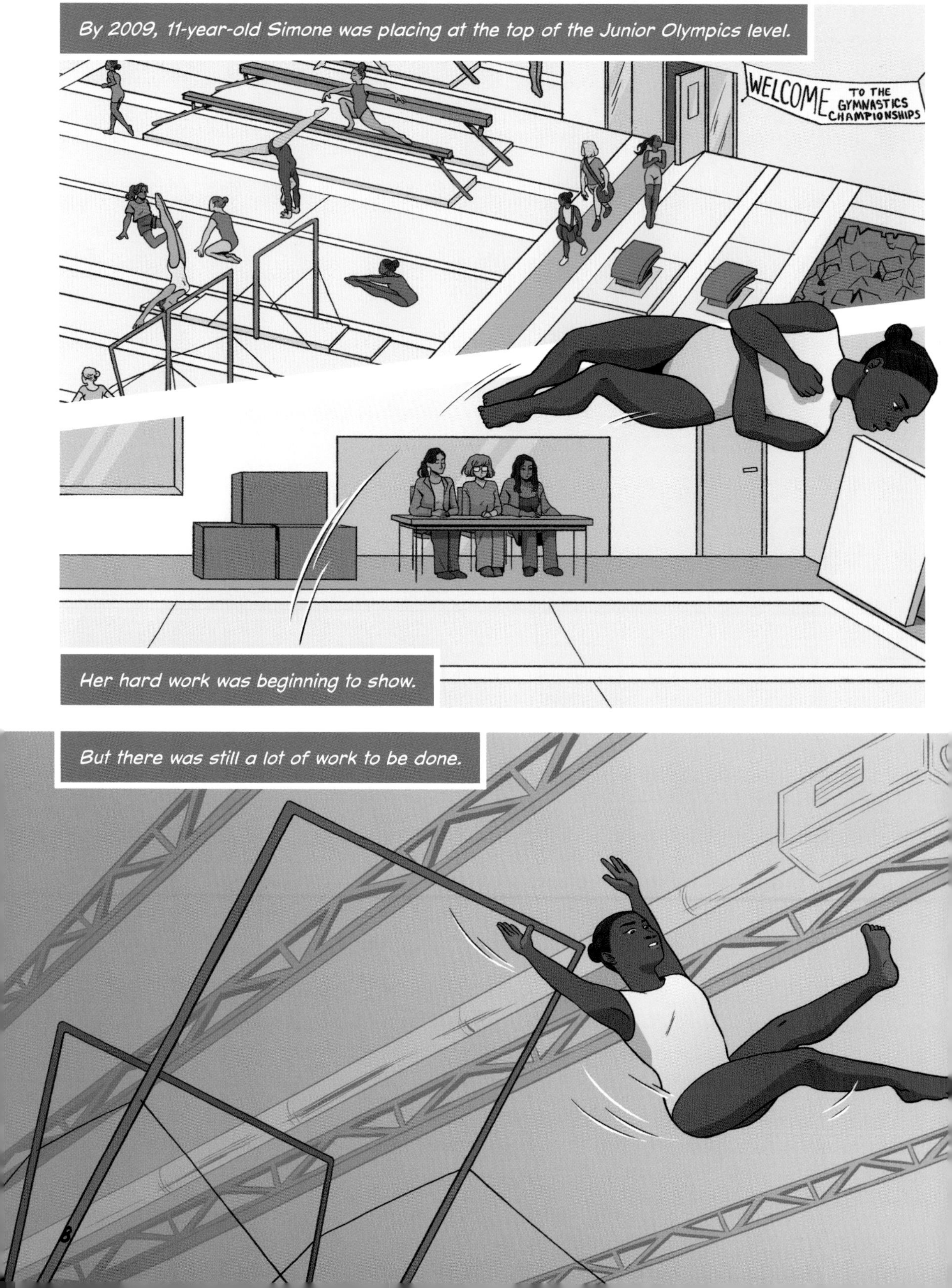
By 2009, 11-year-old Simone was placing at the top of the Junior Olympics level.
WELCOME TO THE GYMNASTICS CHAMPIONSHIPS
Her hard work was beginning to show.
But there was still a lot of work to be done.

Over the next few years, Simone improved. Her competition placings got better and better.

There she goes!

In 2012, Simone switched to schooling at home. The move gave her more time to train.

More training time will help Simone get to the next level.

It paid off. Simone became a top prospect in women's gymnastics.

CHAPTER 2

GAME ON

At 16, Simone qualified to compete in the 2013 Gymnastics World Championships in Antwerp, Belgium.

She won a bronze medal on the balance beam and silver on the vault.

Best of all, she brought home two gold medals. One was for floor exercise. The other gold was the competition's top prize, the individual all-around. This was for a combined high score from all four events.

The next year, Simone went back to the World Championships and dominated the competition. She became the first woman in forty years to win four gold medals at one championship. One gold included an overall team award.

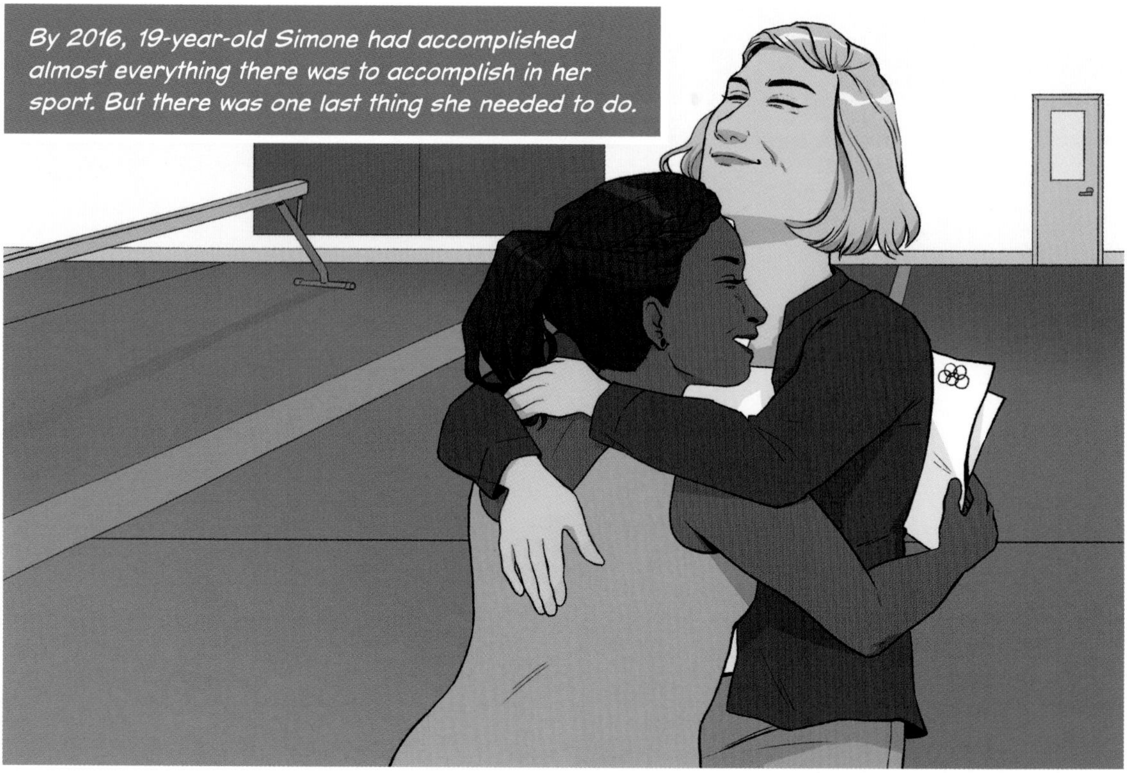
By 2016, 19-year-old Simone had accomplished almost everything there was to accomplish in her sport. But there was one last thing she needed to do.

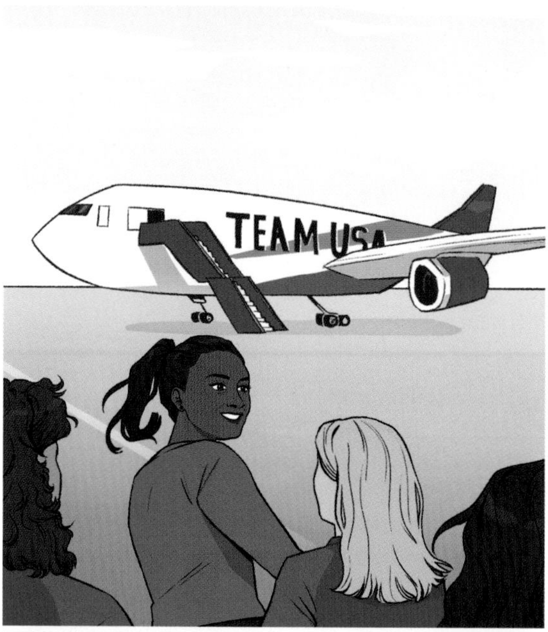
TEAM USA
After her World Championship victories, she joined Team USA at the 2016 Summer Olympics in Rio de Janeiro, Brazil.

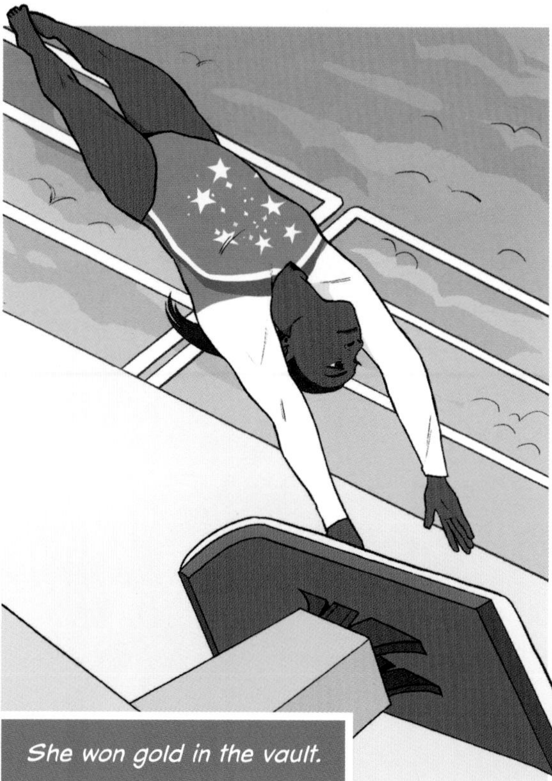
She won gold in the vault.

She also swept the floor exercise.

In the balance beam, she won a bronze medal. But she took home another gold medal in the individual all-around competition.

Simone also led Team USA to victory in the team competition. She was the first American female gymnast ever to win four gold medals at a single Olympic Games.

Less than a month after the Olympics ended, some of Simone's medical records were leaked by Russian hackers.

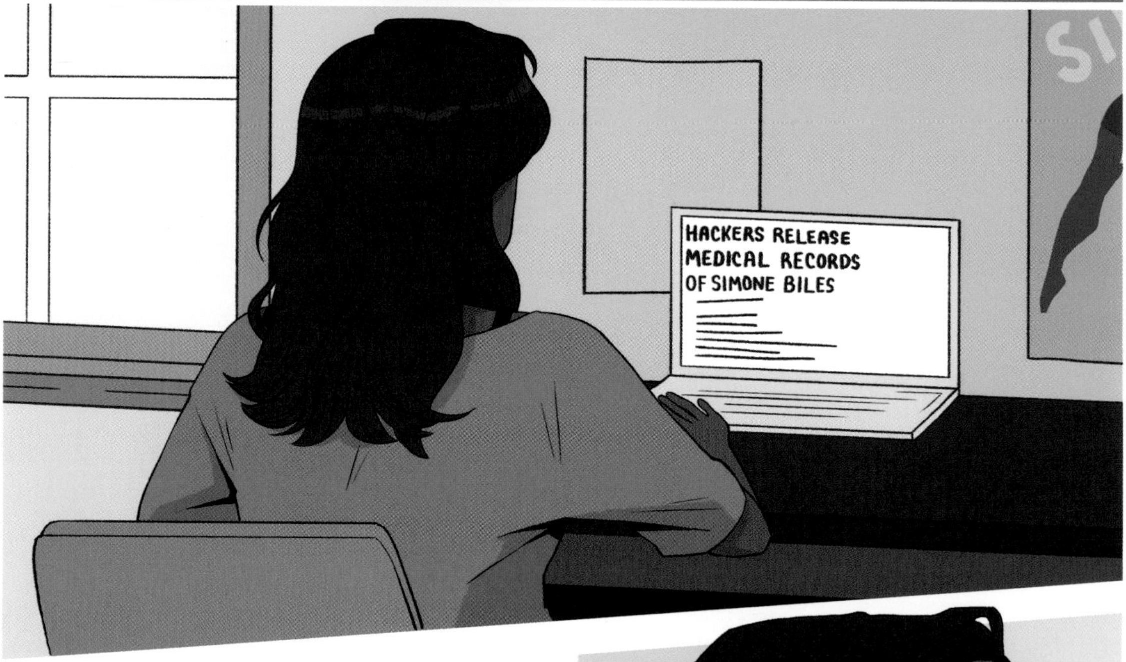
HACKERS RELEASE
MEDICAL RECORDS
OF SIMONE BILES

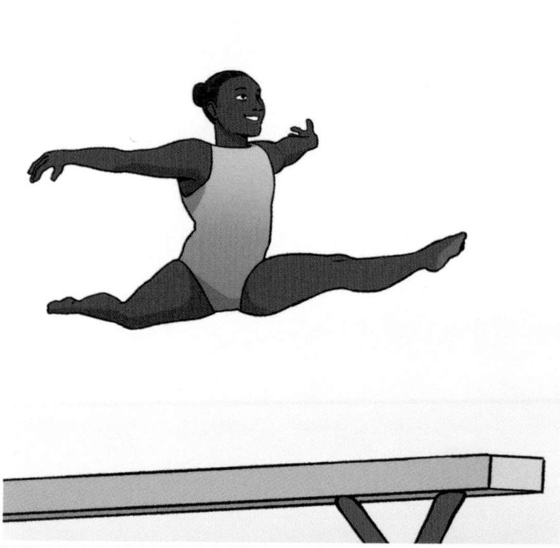

The records showed that Simone took a medicine called Ritalin. The generic name is methylphenidate. She had taken the drug since childhood. It helped with her attention deficit hyperactivity disorder (ADHD). She was able to stay calm and more focused.

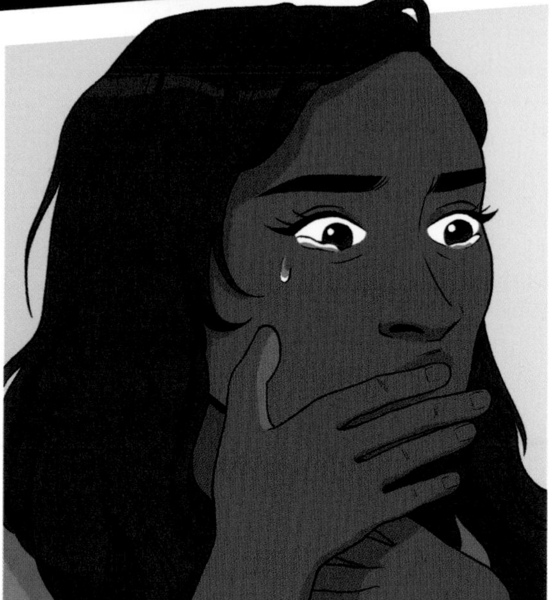

Ritalin is normally not allowed for athletes competing in the Olympics. However, Simone had received special permission. Even though she hadn't done anything wrong, the leak was a painful moment and a massive invasion of her privacy.

Simone had never intended to talk about her struggles with ADHD. But she knew that she was a role model to many. She needed to clear the air.

Maybe I can turn this into something positive.

Simone set her sights on making sure others with ADHD knew that they, too, could achieve greatness.

After that, Simone took the rest of 2016 and 2017 off. She traveled and spent time with family. Simone had been training consistently for more than a decade. Taking a mental health break is something many athletes of the past would not have done. Simone set an example for young people everywhere.

BestSellers

January 8, 2018

| 1 | COURAGE TO SOAR SIMONE BILES |

During her time off, Simone also wrote a book about her life. Readers followed Simone's journey from foster care to the Olympic Games. Her words inspired people across the world.

A break from gymnastics didn't mean a break from competition. In 2017, Simone finished fourth on Dancing with the Stars.

Then in 2018, Simone finally returned to competition. She placed first in every event at the US National Championships.

The World Championships that year were held in Doha, Qatar. The night before, Simone had terrible stomach pains.

Simone went to the emergency room.

Looks like you have a kidney stone.

Will I be okay to compete tomorrow?

I wouldn't suggest it.

Determined to compete, Simone checked herself out of the hospital.

EXIT

The next day.

Simone won four gold medals. She even completed a new move on the vault, which was later named after her. It was a great honor. But it also signaled Simone putting gymnastics ahead of her health.

CHAPTER 3
THE WEIGHT OF THE WORLD

Simone expected her next chance to win Olympic gold to be the 2020 Tokyo Games. These Summer Olympics were pushed to 2021 due to the COVID-19 pandemic. Simone helped the USA qualify for the Team Finals.

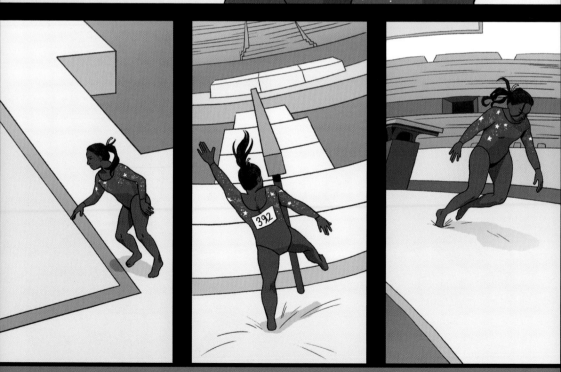

Simone performed, but she made some uncharacteristic mistakes. After qualifying, Simone expressed to her fans on Instagram that she felt the "weight of the world" on her shoulders.

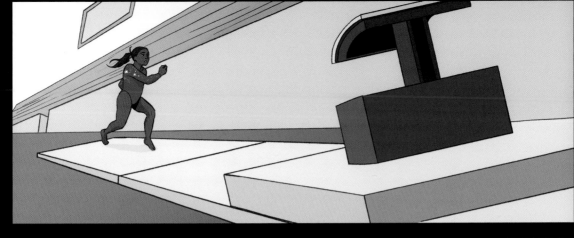

During warm-ups for the final team competition, Simone experienced a phenomenon called the "twisties." The twisties are a temporary inability to do moves a gymnast has done before.

It's like my mind and body aren't communicating with each other.

The twisties struck in the vault competition as well. Simone was unable to complete the routine that she'd planned.

Simone pulled out of the remainder of the team competition. The team won a silver medal without her.

What is wrong with me?

I think we're just a little bit too stressed out, but we should be out here having fun, and sometimes that's not the case.

Simone had to face her teammates. But she also had to face the media.

Why did you pull out of the competition?

I just felt it would be a little bit better to take a back seat, work on my mindfulness. And I knew the girls would do an absolutely great job. And I didn't want to risk the team a medal. . . . They've worked way too hard for that.

Simone pulled out of the first three individual event finals. While her teammates and rivals competed, she worked out in private to see if she could get her mind and body in sync.

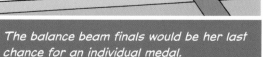

The balance beam finals would be her last chance for an individual medal.

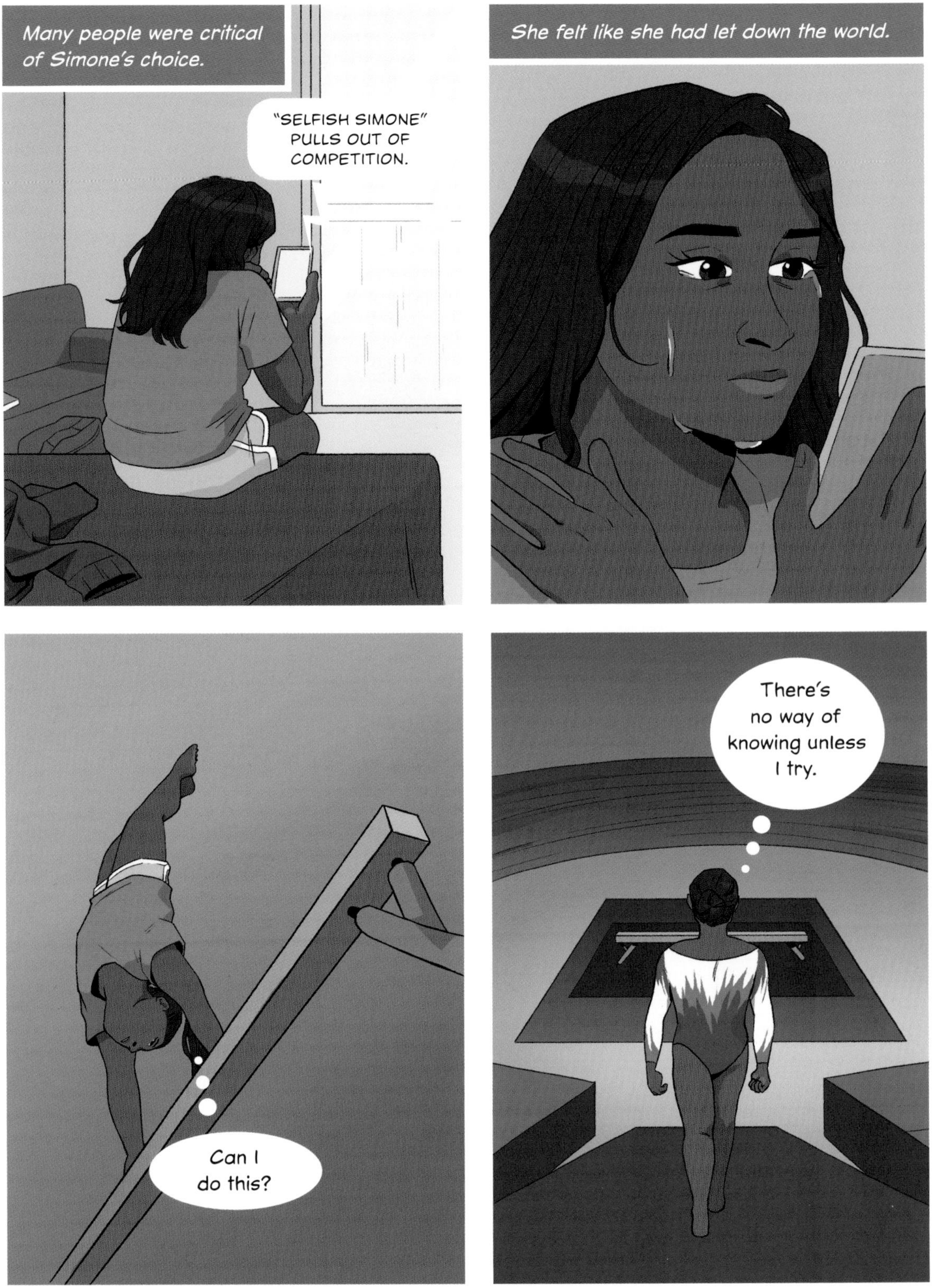
Many people were critical of Simone's choice.
"SELFISH SIMONE" PULLS OUT OF COMPETITION.
She felt like she had let down the world.
Can I do this?
There's no way of knowing unless I try.

Simone made it back to the competition in time for the balance beam finals.

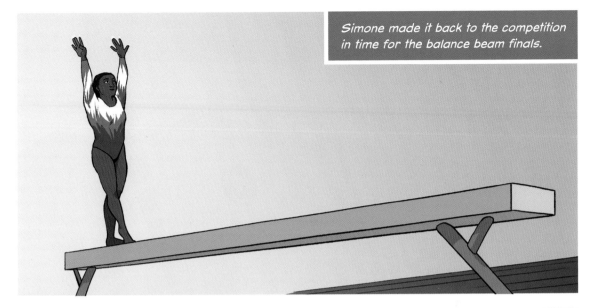

She performed a simpler routine than she'd originally planned. But her program was good enough for a bronze medal.

I'm doing it! ● ● ●

After the Olympics, Simone spoke out about the importance of focusing on mental health.

[The bronze] means more than all of the golds because I've been through so much . . . It was very emotional.

Simone faced another challenging moment later in 2021. Years earlier, a Team USA doctor had committed acts of abuse against Simone and other young gymnasts.

After top USA Gymnastics officials found out, they were slow to act. USA Gymnastics is the sport's governing body. The FBI had failed to investigate claims against the doctor as well. Even so, there was a clear pattern of abuse in women's gymnastics. Many young women suffered.

A few months after the Olympics, Simone was called to testify by the Judiciary Committee of the US Senate. Simone and fellow USA gymnasts McKayla Maroney, Maggie Nichols, and Aly Raisman bravely spoke about the abuses they'd gone through.

Simone and more than 150 other women stepped up.

The organizations created . . . to oversee and protect me as an athlete . . . failed to do their jobs.

Their testimonies led to a 175-year prison sentence for the doctor. American gymnastics would never be the same.

AFTERWORD

The bronze in Tokyo was Simone's seventh Olympic medal. She tied with gymnast Shannon Miller for the most ever by an American woman. She also tied the world record for female gymnasts with 32 combined Olympic and World Championship medals.

By making the decision not to compete in all her events in Tokyo, Simone helped to highlight the mental health struggles that many athletes face. "I say put mental health first," she explained. "Because if you don't, then you're not going to enjoy your sport and you're not going to succeed as much as you want to. So, it's okay sometimes to even sit out the big competitions to focus on yourself. It shows how strong a person and competitor that you really are, rather than just battle through it."

In 2022, Simone received the Presidential Medal of Freedom. This is the highest honor given to Americans who are not in the military. She was the youngest person ever to receive the award.

While she is not retired, she is taking time to focus on her mental health instead of competing. In August 2023, she returned to the competition world. Fans sold out the stadium to show their support. Simone won easily, earning top scores for difficult moves.

ATHLETE SNAPSHOT

BIRTH NAME: Simone Arianne Biles

NICKNAME: $imoney

BORN: March 14, 1997

Awards of Note

◆ Most decorated US women's gymnast ever

◆ 2014–2015–United States Olympic Committee Female Olympic Athlete of the Year

◆ 2021–*TIME* magazine's 100 Most Influential People

◆ 2022–Presidential Medal of Freedom

◆ 2022–*USA Today* Women of the Year Honoree

SOURCE NOTES

22   Orlana Gonzalez, "Simone Biles Pulls Out of Team Finals to Focus on Mental Health," *Axios*, July 27, 2001, https://www.axios.com/2021/07/27/simone-biles-gymnastics-finals-injury-mental-health

23   Bill Chappell, "Read What Simone Biles Said After Her Withdrawal From the Olympic Finals," *NPR*, July 28, 2021, https://www.npr.org/sections/tokyo-olympics-live-updates/2021/07/28/1021683296/in-her-words-what-simone-biles-said-after-her-withdrawal

25   "Simone Biles on Her Beam Bronze: 'It Means More Than All the Golds'," *Olympics.com*, October 5, 2021, https://olympics.com/en/news/gymnastics-simone-biles-beam-bronze-tokyo-social-media-reaction

27   Rose Minutaglio, "Simone Biles Wants Answers About the FBI's Larry Nassar Investigation," *Yahoo!*, September 16, 2021, https://www.yahoo.com/now/simone-biles-wants-answers-fbi-160700109.html

GLOSSARY

addiction: a treatable medical disease that involves habit-forming behavior

attention deficit hyperactivity disorder: a condition that includes difficulty paying attention, hyperactivity, and impulsiveness

dismount: leaving a piece of equipment at the end of a routine

finesse: delicate and refined

foster home: a place where children are brought up by someone other than their parent

hacker: a person who uses computers to gain information or achieve a goal

mindfulness: the practice of living in the moment

suburb: an area outside a city where people live

testify: to give evidence as a witness in a court of law

FURTHER INFORMATION

Britannica Kids: Simone Biles
https://kids.britannica.com/kids/article/Simone-Biles/634111

Sabelko, Rebecca. *Simone Biles*. Minneapolis: Bellwether Media, 2023.

Schwartz, Heather E. *Simone Biles: Greatest of All Time*. Minneapolis: Lerner Publications, 2023.

SI Kids: Simone Biles
https://www.sikids.com/tag/simone-biles

Smith, Elliott. *Black Achievements in Sports: Celebrating Fitz Pollard, Simone Biles, and More*. Minneapolis: Lerner Publications, 2024.

TIME For Kids: This is Simone
https://www.timeforkids.com/g56/this-is-simone-biles/

INDEX